Intimate Worship Songs and Poems

By Oluwakemi Odujinrin

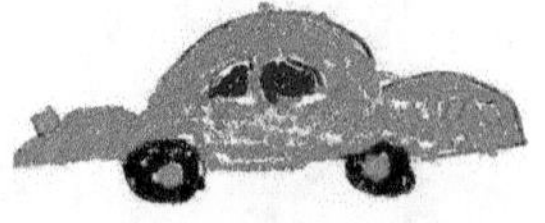

Alpha Car Self-Publishing

ISBN-13: 978-1-78808-046-0

Dedication

This book is dedicated to my family, particularly my children because they are the future and they need to be taught how to worship God the creator. This book is for Teni, Temi, and Tomi because they challenge me all the time to step up, be a true worshipper, and be an example.

I also want to give thanks to God who always leads me triumphantly, so that when life is difficult, I am not disillusioned and I believe I can live a victorious life every day. It is only a matter of our mindset.

This book is also dedicated to all worshippers who know that it is an effort to be in sync with God in our rather complex world.

Purpose

I started writing many of these songs twelve years ago. I have compiled them to showcase the amazing things that can cross our minds under pressure, and especially to show that God still inspires people. You need only to open yourself to Him, and all that He can express through us is endless. This book is designed to glorify God and to touch the lives of anyone who may be going through any kind of challenging situation so that they can be encouraged and have the strength to carry on.

Our problems, I believe, are only as large as the attention we choose to give to them. It is possible to be positive in a difficult time, and it is also fine to acknowledge that when we are finding things difficult, we need the help of God and of others.

This book can appeal to young people who want to know more about the Lord, and parents who want to teach their children how to worship the Lord because such is important and is a mark of a good and developing Christian.

This book will appeal to people who just want to tap into a very intimate resource for uplifting their spirits and enjoy the depths of any relationship that can exist between God and ordinary people who seek Him.

Oluwakemi Odujinrin

Content

Songs to the Lord

Sing unto the Lord a new song, let His praises fill this temple.

 # The Answer

It is a long road, when you feel you cannot do it all alone then Jesus comes your way and He sets you free.

He is the answer to the world today; He is the healer of all that is worth healing each day.

He is the answer to the heartfelt cry of that person in dire straits right now, the helper of those who need Him just now.

You should know that He is the one who can lift you up as He works in your life with His comforting Spirit.

July 1999

# *Give it to the ancient of days*

To Him who is the old man of worth, the ancient of days, give it all up to Him.

Give praise, give Him glory and honor. To Him give all adoration.

Love Him as he is the beginning and the end. We have to praise the King for all He has done in our lives.

Low and behold, the trumpet sounds that Jesus Christ is Lord. Tossing and turning through hurts and pain, He's always there for us.

22nd November 1999

 *No one*

No one can stop the work of God in our lives.

No one can stop God's work regarding us, his saints.

As I walk through the valley of the shadow of death, I fear no evil. As you do the work of the Lord and face all opposition.

No one can stop the work of God in our lives.

As you stand in the congregation of His people to praise.

No one can stop the work of God in our lives.

17th November 1999

I have come

I have come to bring You a song offering and to give You the great worship that You deserve.

I have come with a token from my heart to show You how much I appreciate You Lord.

I was walking down a lonely road all by myself until the day you came and You set me free. No words can describe Your loving kindness in my life. I have come to sing of how much I love You Lord.

17ᵗʰ January 2000

You are the one

Lord, You let me know You, since I knew You I have been filled.

In so many ways I cannot explain, You hold the key to my life and all I ever really wanted is in You.

Your goodness surely baffles me; You are all in all and a friend indeed, I need You Lord, I love You Lord, Let the whole world know that Your mightiness fills the whole earth.

23rd January 2000

# *I surrender all*

I surrender all my troubles at Your feet Lord. With Your help, I can carry on in troubled times.

You have promised to stand by us in our sorrows, all we need to do is put our trust in You.

I surrender all to You with the knowledge that you make everything safe.

I gave my all to You walking by faith and not by sight and surrender all.

7th February 2000

 *I have never known a love like Yours before*

Lord, I have no reason to doubt Your love for me.

You have created me in Your own special way. Gently, Your love flows right through You to me. It has made me to be the very best and as I lift my voice and sing, I vow to do what you want me to do.

I have never known a love like yours before.

February 14, 2000

God's people

We are all God's people born of the Holy Spirit.

Let the glory of the Lord come down so we can praise. Alleluia praise Him for He is worthy, praise Him for he's good, praise him for he's wonderful and you would never be the same again.

Born of God we are blessed, consecrated by the blood, let's go brethren to the Lord with all, so we can praise.

21st – 22nd February 2000

Wonderfully and fearfully

Made that is what I am.

I am convinced that Your love is all I need.

You made me in Your image when You formed the Earth through all things; I know Your comfort is always there as You made me. Wonderfully and fearfully made, that's what I am.

You were the rock of my salvation when I was lost. You knew me before I was born.

It is in Your word; now I know my steps were ordered by You, as You made me.

22nd February 2000

 *Be merciful*

Be merciful to me O God for my soul trusts in You. In the shadow of Your wings I take my refuge.

I will cry to You the most high God because You do all things for me and You shall send help from heaven to save me, to reproach all those who want to swallow me.

God shall send forth His mercies and His truth when I lie among the sons of men who are set on fire.

You do all things for me,

You stand from Heaven to save me; to reproach all those who want to swallow me.

22nd February 2000

 *Peace of God*

I have got a mission to come to tell you that the peace of God is here with you. You have gone so far, that you feel the peace is not here with you. If you move too far away, He cannot shield you under the shadow of His majesty, but I know the Lord will give you peace if you dwell in Him.

The peace of the Lord; it knows no bounds and it is the only peace you should know because there is no other.

22ⁿᵈ February 2000

 ## *Burn in me*

Let the fire of God burn in you so that you can be what the Lord wants you to be.

Let it burn in you so that you can do what

He wants you to do. Look around you as the days go by knowing you have work to do. Depression sets in and our spirit just wants to drag then, I know I cannot do anything by myself.

So, let the Lord take control as His fire burns in you.

22nd February 2000

You are my Lord

Christ Jesus wonderful savior to me, You are my all in all and I worship You, Lord of lords, wonderful counselor to me I praise Your holy name irreverently.

You are my Lord, I bless Your holy name, my Lord, I give You all the glory today, I give You all the glory today.

Lord of Lords wonderful counselor to me, I bless Your holy name in Majesty.

You are my Lord, I bless Your holy name, my Lord, I give You all the glory today, I give You all the glory today.

15th March 2001

 *Blood of Jesus*

The blood of Jesus freed me from my sins and more. It showed me that I could be what He wants me to be. The name of Jesus is higher than all other names; it gives me strength that I can overcome always.

The words of Jesus show me the way to go in doing all I have set out to do.

The thoughts of God written by His holy men let me know how to live my life.

Although I have made mistakes, I fall and rise again and though troubles last for awhile, joy comes in the morning.

2001

 *He will be*

Beautiful God beyond compare Once He touches you, you will never be the same.

When the scales fall from your eyes, like they fell from the eyes of Paul, then you begin to see life from a whole new angle.

Beautiful God beyond compare

The only one who can do what no man can do.

He lets you know where you should go.

What you have been doing for twenty years,

God can make possible in a day, and you will start to know that He is the provider. Riches and wealth are illusions. Unless those in the Spirit according to the word of the living God, who gives and takes as He pleases, never leaving you empty of what you will need.

Turn to Him and you will see we serve a living God who goes into battle just for you. He will be all you will ever need.

He will be your father

He will be your brother

He will be your sister

He will be your friend

He will be everything.

30th August 2001

Give a little thought

Have you ever seen green grass grow without rain?

Have you ever seen the day go without night or break of dawn?

Have you ever seen the moon in the day or the sun at night?

Have you ever seen cloudless skies?

Were any of these made by man?

They were made for you and me.

What would it be like if we did not have what we have now?

Give a little thought to what you do each day.

Appreciate the time you have to spend and make the most of it because you only live once!

23rd December 2001

 *The Lord was with me*

I was attacked in my dream; nothing in my mind could see what was in it.

I thought I was going to lose my mind but I checked and the Lord was with me.

Even though it seemed so dark;

Dreams of woe, of death and a depraved mind.

I thought I was going to lose my mind but I checked and the Lord was in it.

January 2004

 *Lamb of God*

Lamb of God who was given to take the sins of the Lord away.

Holy one solely devoted to the mission He had been sent.

He felt truly forsaken as He turned to the father. At the cross He gave His life and for all was crucified.

Jesus is Lord.

Master of all things

Greater than anything

That you could ever dream

He has risen

Now we have eternity

The Lamb of God.

April 2009

 *In my troubles*

In my troubles, I looked all around me and I saw, there was nowhere to turn to so I turned to the Lord explicitly.

He made a way where there was none, comforted me in a wary place; He did just what His word said.

He was with me never leaving nor forsaking.

2010

 *Just a closer walk*

Just a closer walk with thee is all I need to get through this situation of mine, just a closer walk with thee.

You know that situations come to test you, no matter the condition you find yourself in, you must know about your God, that He is there for always, anytime you feel dismayed, you just say:

Just a closer walk with the.....

2010

Poems to the Lord

Praising the Lord Praise Him
In His Sanctuary
Praise Him
In the firmament of His Power.

 *A new day, a new dawn*

It is a new day, yes a new dawn. The light is shining and we are hoping for the ray of hope being drawn from the sight of the piping that is the Spirit which links us.

To the Lord who reigns almighty? Check is He really in thy heart 'Cos it is crucial in the coming to Resist and Submit in the way it ought to be.

It is yet a new day, a new dawn the light whence shining but the hope is now come.

2009

Who is the Lord?

Who is the Lord? It is our God

What are His ways?

They are strong, they are mighty.

Who is the Lord?

It is our God

What are His Ways?

They are awesome and they are faithful.

Who is the Lord? It is our God

What are His Ways?

Wonderful, Glorious, and Marvelous!

May 2011

 *I look*

I look to my left and right and see the people of God plan a vain thing.

Their eyes blinded by the promise of more from this person who is unable to bless like our God.

They grovel and familiarize. They show loyalty to a point of anomaly. They however disdain the chosen and anointed of God.

The Lord says touch not my anointed, do my prophet no harm. Who then is able to bless like our God and establish like the Lord? Trust in Him only because men only plan a vain thing.

May 2011

 *My breaking heart*

In my distress, I share with God my heart as it seems to be breaking.

His Word says, he that dwells in the secret place shall abide under the shadow of Him who is able to deliver from all aches.

How the Lord shelters me at such times and I know nothing can touch me.

My breaking heart is still, it trusts in the Lord.

It is hopeful knowing God is the hope of my heart's salvation.

In my distress, it is okay to feel pain knowing He will take it away and I will never know it anymore.

May 2011

 *True Word*

Lord, your word is true because You desire to meet with Your people in praise and adoration.

You are the mighty God, with whom words are not enough to express. Lord, your word is true because You desire to meet with Your people in praise and adulation.

Let Your name be praised forever more as you accept our humble praise.

Lord, your word is true because You desire to meet with Your people in praise and expectation.

The name of the Lord is glorified in all things.

May 2011

 *You are God*

In my distress, I look to the Lord for direction.

I sometimes wonder how You speak to me, as I sometimes feel a tightening in my stomach and a sensing in my Spirit.

How will I know you are there?

You are like a mighty flood in your answers and sometimes like a mild wind.

You are God, no matter what life may bring. You are strong even when we seem weak.

Continue to love us to know You in Your fullness where no holds can stop us and other things pale in comparison to you.

May 2011

Meaningfulness

Strong and mighty and beautiful Lord.

You are the manifestation of meaningfulness in life, the Lord of hosts.

You are the Lord who speaks and the Lord who knows all things.

When we open ourselves up to You, we know peace, joy, greatness, life abundant, testimonies, and all things.

Let us know You for sound mind, deliverances, and healings continuously because they are who You are.

May 2011

 *In Your name*

In Your name, we win battles.

In Your name, we take the lands.

In Your name, we harness the future.

In Your name, we are inventive. In Your name, we are creative.

In Your name, we rise when we fall.

In Your name, we defeat our adversaries. In your name, we conquer our foes.

In Your name, we are delivered from all troubles.

In the name of our Lord, we are blessed and can lift-up our banner.

May 2011

 *Creator*

With you we find answers in the time of need.

You are the beautiful God and I trust in you.

Heathens will come to know and serve you because you are the creator of the heavens and the earth.

May 2011

 *Angels*

The angels of the Lord are at work in the life of the believer.

Call on the Lord and He will send the angels through the Spirit of the living God.

Call on the Lord, you His peoples, find time for Him, and consecrate yourself unto the Lord because He is our help.

May 2011

 *Bless Him*

Bless Him, bless Him, bless Him. In the congregation of His peoples. In the workplace, bless Him.

In troubles, bless Him.

With your children, bless Him.

Bless Him everywhere. Bless Him always.

May 2011

 *Lead me*

Lord, you lead me in your triumph, Lord.

I can rely on the Lord at all times.

There is no end to your greatness. We will continually and always have reason to worship you.

Your goodness and mercy fills the earth.

May 2011

 *In the darkness*

In my darkness, I saw myself being chased by a dark form.

There were monsters all around me and I called on the Lord. I said, 'holy!'

The heavens opened and the waters rose and covered my enemies.

He made nothing of them and I went away safe.

May 2011

 *Gloom*

Dogs chased me, hyenas around me, looking to devour me.

Gloom and doom encompassed me as I saw no way out. I could only see what the day could bring, but in my heart I knew only God could deliver. I called to him and he answered.

His word said to take heart, to wait on Him and He will strengthen my heart.

He did.

May 2011

 *Judgment*

In the skies, I saw the judgment scale of God and I knew I had to make a choice to serve Him or not.

It was a dark night, but the Lord was clear in His asking and guidance and I chose the Lord of hosts as master and as King over my life.

Not one day has passed that I regret knowing you Lord.

In a dream with angels I met with the judge who had to declare me chosen or cornered.

Not one day has passed that I regret knowing you Lord.

May 2011

The Lord speaks

The Lord speaks even in a desert place.

He speaks His heart to your heart.

If you will listen, you will hear Him comforting, hear him saying I want to talk with you and to walk with you; I want to hold your hand and lead you so you will not stumble and fall.

The Lord speaks and you will hear Him, if you listen.

June 2011

 *Let me know you more*

Lord let me know you more.

The cry of my heart is to know you more and make your deeds and ways known in our world today. Many times, I feel it is not enough to have knowledge of You but rather to have a true moment with You……., a meaningful moment of joy and peace.

An experiential moment of peace with no cares of this world invading.

June 2011

 *Persecutions*

Persecutions come our way because we serve you Lord.

We are misunderstood and underestimated.

We are lied upon and falsely accused and we are not allowed an opinion even when everyone else has an opinion about us.

We must be politically 'correct' in an incorrect world of conformists.

The need to be patient amidst the desire to be a tyrant.

These and more will not stop us from praising and worshipping Your holy name Lord God.

June 2011

 *Our God*

Then, it came about that our God has proved Himself to be magnificent through His deeds of creation, allocation, contribution, continuation, and redemption.

Dagon of the Philistines could not stand before him or any of the gods being worshipped today, and in the times to come.

June 2011

Praise and Worship

Praising the Lord brings joy to my heart; it fills my heart with extreme gladness that I can worship the Lord at all times.

Praising the Lord is a good thing because when the praises go up, His blessings come raining down.

Praising the Lord is not a feeling, it is an action that should be indulged in as a routine of worship, and an exclamation of joy that encompasses fully.

June 2011

 *Adversity*

Adversity comes once again, what am I to do? I call on you and seek your face, my helper and redeemer. Who is there like you?

June 2011

Arise O Lord

Arise oh Lord and let my enemies be confused.

They plan to take over my life and make me miserable, but I hope in my God, the source of my salvation. You are worthy of all my praise.

June 2011

 *Are You not the Lord?*

Are You not the Lord who does great things?

Yet again, You have stilled the hand of the enemies over my life; You have not allowed me to fulfill the expectations of my enemies.

You have lifted me up, answered my prayers, and shown that you are indeed God all by yourself.

June 2011

 *This morning*

I woke up this morning very confident that my day will be meaningful.

That evil will no longer be my portion, and that You are always there to save.

Even though I was tired, I knew You would bless me in the morning, afternoon, and night.

All day long, You would bless me.

June 2011

 *Lord of Hosts*

Bless the Lord of hosts because He is worthy.

He is righteous and able to save and deliver.

He is the mighty King of kings and holy Lord of lords.

Our God is great beyond measure;

He is able to achieve much for you. Put your trust in the Lord and He will elevate you to greater heights.

Bless the Lord of hosts because He is worthy.

June 2011

Children of light

Children of light, appeal to the Lord for guidance.

Be responsible for walking continuously in the light of God. Know that there is no joy in the world but in the presence of God, there is fullness of joy and at His right hand, there are pleasures evermore.

June 2011

 ## The ways of the Lord

The ways of the Lord are perfect and His testimony pure.

When poverty came knocking I said to him, 'the Lord rebuke you'. Untimely death came and I said, 'the Lord has made you my footstool and I refuse to go'.

When sickness came, I looked to the Lord and His word and sickness had to go.

The ways of the Lord are perfect and he had given me a testimony.

June 2011

Solitary

God has set up the solitary in families for greatness, saying 'He has given meaning to my life and let me be the apple of His eye'.

He will lift you up and take all your pain away.

He will make you a great nation. Just trust in Him.

June 2011

 *Lift-up your hands*

Lift-up your hands in the congregation of the peoples and bless the Lord.

Give Him praise and bless Him with your mouth with your heart so pure.

Bless the Lord with your children; bless him with your spouse.

Lift-up your hands in the congregation of the people and bless Him.

June 2011

 *Teach your children*

Teach your children to walk in the way of the Lord from when they are born.

Be an example to them in your praise and in your worship.

Tell them of the good deeds which the Lord has done for you and for others.

Children ought to know the Lord from when they are young.

May the Lord be praised as we suffer the little children to come unto Him.

June 2011

 *Young people ought to praise the Lord*

In the house of God, young people ought to praise the Lord. Parents, teach your children to praise the Lord.

It is their heritage from you to know the Lord of hosts because He is all for the cause of them that serve Him and take the time to know Him. Teach your young children to know the Lord so it may be well with them all their days.

June 2011

He will bring you out

In a dark place, you can trust the Lord because He will bring you out. He will cause your hard place to become soft and let you know the power of His glory.

It is easy to think there is no way out when it is hard, but do not be discouraged because the Lord can be with you in a difficult place and make you an overcomer.

Just lean on Him and trust in Him and He will make it good.

June 2011

 *Do not be dismayed*

Do not be dismayed when even in the house of God; they call you names because the devil even cons and deceives in God's house.

As you call in Him and intercede for others, His light will come and take out all darkness.

June 2011

 *About the Author*

My name is Oluwakemi (Kemi) Odujinrin.

I am a writer, poet, song writer, singer, and worship leader in a church choir. I have published these songs and poems to share with others my level of worship of the Lord over the years, how this has impacted my life positively in so many ways, and how it can change a person for the better.

I am married and I have three beautiful children.

www.ingramcontent.com/pod-product-compliance
Lightning Source LLC
Chambersburg PA
CBHW051010050726
47592CB00007B/2782